D1499425

The Little Kid's

AMERICANA

Craft Book

Jackie Vermeer

The Little Kid's
AMERICANA
Craft Book

Photography by Duane D. Davis

Taplinger Publishing Company • *New York*

By Jackie Vermeer and Marian Lariviere
THE LITTLE KID'S CRAFT BOOK
THE LITTLE KID'S FOUR SEASONS CRAFT BOOK

First Edition

Published in the United States in 1975 by
TAPLINGER PUBLISHING CO., INC.
New York, New York

Published simultaneously in the Dominion of Canada by
Burns & MacEachern, Ltd., Toronto

Library of Congress Catalog Card Number: 74-21698

ISBN 0-8008-4927-2

2-76

To my Mother

ACKNOWLEDGMENTS

I sincerely thank the wonderful people who have been so generous in sharing their ideas. Thank you to the children who allowed me to use their work. I am grateful to Duane Davis for his excellent photography. And a very special thank you to my husband, Lou, and my children, David and Kristi, who have so willingly helped, in so many ways, to make this all possible.

All color and black and white photography by Duane D. Davis, with the exception of photographs on pages 52 and 93, which are by Paul McMaster. All drawings and illustrations are by the author.

CONTENTS

*This collection of activities was adapted for children
from American folk crafts. It is offered in the hope of
providing opportunities for children to develop their
creative and inventive talents. The main purpose is for
them to have fun, and if they learn a bit of history
in the process, so much the better.*

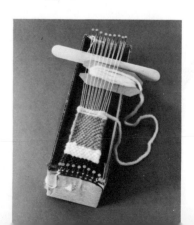

9

ILLUSTRATIONS IN COLOR

The Little Kid's
AMERICANA
Craft Book

1.
Paper Play

The availability of paper, even in Colonial days, made it a common material for craft use. Quilling is one of the paper crafts, popular during those early days, which children of today will most certainly enjoy. Strips of paper, scissors, and a bit of glue are the only supplies needed to do quilling, a technique used to create delightful three-dimensional designs and pictures.

Quilling is simply rolled strips of paper placed so as to form a design. Most any kind of lightweight paper can be used for the strips. Cut the strips about one-half inch wide, and at least 6 inches in length. Quilling was generally done with much narrower strips, but the wider strips are more easily handled by children.

Quilled flower

*Quilling and
a felt-pen drawing*

The technique is simple. The child rolls the paper strip tightly around a pencil or paintbrush handle and then releases it. The strip will unroll a bit. It can be used as it is, or the end of the strip can be glued against the curl. The roll can be used in its circular form, or be pinched or bent into different shapes. The child can arrange the rolls on a construction-paper background and glue them in place. For

Gluing the end
against the curl

variety, have strips of colored paper or use the rolled strips to accentuate felt-pen drawings.

A delightful frame for these pictures can be made from a flat box (hosiery or lingerie box). A background paper is cut to fit inside the box and glued in place. The design is then added and a piece of yarn attached to the back for hanging.

Quilled butterfly made from colored paper strips,
displayed in a box frame

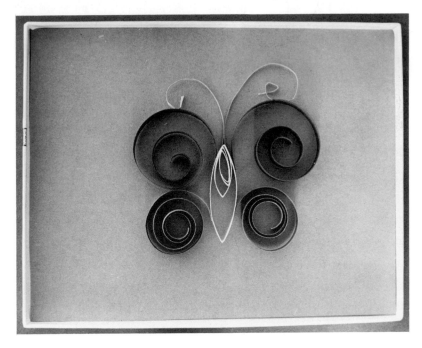

Paper cutting, known by such tongue-twisting names as Scheren-schnitte and Papyrotamia, requires only paper and scissors. Here, a design is cut from a piece of folded paper. Most children are familiar with this technique, as they have cut valentines in this fashion, but any object or design will work as long as some portion of the fold is left uncut. Newspaper and typing paper are good for beginners, as they are easy to cut. Later you may want to use colored construction paper.

Encourage the child to try a variety of shapes, but remind him to be sure to leave some portion of the fold uncut. Some of his favorite cut-paper pieces can be mounted on a dark-colored background. A small cutting glued onto a piece of folded construction paper makes an unusual greeting card.

Cut-paper greeting cards

This procedure can be carried one step further by making more folds in the paper. Fold the paper in half, and then in half again on a parallel line. This will give three folds. The design is then cut,

Series of designs cut from three folds

leaving a portion of each side uncut. This opens into a series of connected designs.

The most familiar result of this type of folding and cutting is a row of paper dolls. It is fascinating for children to watch as the cut paper is unfolded and all the dolls appear holding hands. Of course, this need not be limited to dolls—flowers, trees, or any other symmetrical design works as well. For the dolls, the paper is folded

Cutting paper dolls,
with the center line on
the fold line

in half three times, and half of the doll shape is cut out. In this case, the center line of the doll, or other design, will be on the fold line.

Paper dolls

Snowflakes can be cut in this same manner, but the paper must be folded differently. You will need to help the child fold the paper the first few times. Using a regular-size (8½″ x 11″) piece of typing paper, first fold it in half crosswise, and then into thirds. To make the fold even, mark the center of the fold line, then measure 1⅛″ inches from the upper right corner of the paper. Lay a ruler along the two marks, then fold over the right edge of the paper, making a fold along the edge of the ruler. Take the left edge and fold it over the first. Fold in half once again and cut off the upper uneven portion, 4 inches from the point.

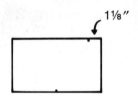

1. Mark the center of the fold line. Measure 1⅛″ from the corner. Lay a ruler between the two points to make the fold line.

2. Right side folded over.

3. Left side folded over.

Six-pointed snowflakes

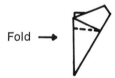

Fold ➜

4. Fold in half again. Cut off upper portion 4 inches from the point.

This folding produces the six-pointed shape that is typical of a snowflake. As with the paper dolls, the fold line is the center line of each snowflake point. The more cuts thàt are made into the paper, the lacier the snowflake will be. Each one is new and different and

Variations of snowflake cutting

fascinating. These snowflakes can be used to decorate windows in winter as they were many years ago.

To the early Americans, silhouettes were an inexpensive alternative for having one's portrait painted. A silhouette is actually a paper shadow. To make a child's silhouette, you will first need to produce his shadow by means of a strong light. A large flashlight, at a distance of ten feet, gives a good, clear shadow, but you may wish to experiment with other types of lighting. Just remember that a sharp shadow is essential here. Have the child stand or sit close to a wall, facing either to the right or left. Tape or tack a piece of white drawing paper on the wall behind his head. Then quickly sketch the outline of his head. The outline is cut out and can be mounted on black paper.

Silhouettes

True silhouettes are black, just like the shadows. If you wish to make a black one, use the white outline as a pattern to cut a new one from black paper. These can then be mounted on white paper. These silhouettes make a perfect gift for a parent or grandparent.

Folding paper is a very old art form, and one children particularly enjoy. To seem to make something from nothing is especially appealing to youngsters. By folding a square piece of paper, a child can make a picture frame or a box. It is best to start with a lightweight paper until he has learned the procedure, then perhaps he will want to try a heavier paper—particularly for the box. In any case, he will surely want to make several of each as they are such fun to do. The frames can be used for photographs, dried flowers, or a small drawing. The folded boxes make an unusual way to wrap small gifts or party favors.

You may wish to have the child start with the folded paper frame, as it is the easier of the two. This will give him a little experience before starting on the box. You can use any size square, but an 8-inch square is easily handled by a beginner.

TO MAKE A PAPER FRAME:

1. Using a square piece of paper, fold diagonally and open. Fold diagonally in the opposite direction and open.
2. Fold all corners over the center, and keep folded.
3. Turn the paper over and again fold each corner to the center, and keep folded.
4. Turn the paper over again, and fold the tips of the paper back to the corners to form the frame.

Folded-paper frames

5. Insert the photograph or drawing.
6. The folds on the back side will unfold a bit, so as to prop up the frame. If you wish a flat frame, tape the tips in place.

    For a two-colored frame, use two squares of paper in different colors. Lay one on top of the other, and fold as one piece.

TO FOLD A PAPER BOX:

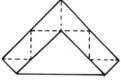

1. Using a square piece of paper, fold diagonally and open. Fold diagonally in the opposite direction and open.
2. Fold each tip to the center and open.
3. Fold each tip to the upper fold line and open. Fold lines are shown by dotted lines.

4. Fold each tip to the bottom fold line and open.

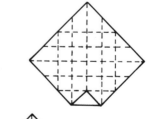

5. Cut out the two triangle shapes on each edge (8 in all). These are shown by the arrows in the diagram.

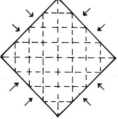

Folded-paper boxes. The box at the left is at the stage where a small favor can be inserted.

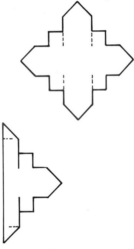

6. Cut down the length of one block, as shown by the dotted lines in the diagram.

7. Fold the paper in half, and cut a slot to form tabs in the opposite ends, at the first fold line. Fold over the edges of the tab so it will slip into the slot easily. Unfold, and repeat this with the other two ends.

8. Taking two opposite corners, bring them together and slip the tab into the slot. Unfold the tab edges so it will stay in place. The box is now taking shape. If desired, a small gift or favor can now be slipped inside the box. Bring up the other two sides, tuck the flaps in, and slip the tab into the slot. Again unfold the tab edges so it will stay in place.

Reverse painting on a sheet of clear acetate

Reverse painting on glass was, at one time, a very popular method of painting. Here, a picture was painted directly on a piece of glass. When finished the glass was turned over and framed. Of course, when the glass was turned over, the picture was reversed. Any words or letters on the painting had to be painted backwards so that they were readable when the painting was turned over.

Children can do a form of reverse painting using sheets of acetate (a clear plastic sheeting). The picture is drawn on one side of the acetate with felt markers. The drawing is then turned over and placed on a construction-paper background of a contrasting color. A construction-paper frame completes the picture. Children will be delighted to find that their finished picture appears to be covered with real glass.

Tinsel painting, a variation of reverse painting on glass, was done in much the same way. In this case a layer of tinfoil, or tinsel, was placed behind the picture. This background was allowed to show through in some areas of the painting, and gave an added dimension to the picture.

Tinsel painting

To make a tinsel picture, the child first paints his picture on a piece of acetate with felt markers. The areas of color made by the markers tend to lose their distinctive shapes when placed against the reflecting foil background. To prevent this, it is best to outline the drawing with a black marker. For the background, the child will need a piece of cardboard or stiff paper the same size as the acetate, and a piece of aluminum foil several inches larger than the cardboard. The foil should be crumpled and then carefully smoothed out. Glue the foil to the cardboard and trim any excess at the edges. The final step is to place the picture on the foil, reversing the picture so that the painted side is next to the foil. Staple on a construction-paper frame, or use colored tape around the edges. The colored tape is particularly good since it not only frames the picture, but also serves to hold the layers together.

A foil background also produces an unusual effect when used with colored cut-paper designs. The design is glued to the foil, then covered with a sheet of acetate. Strips of colored tape provide the frame. This is a good way to make a Halloween picture, as the foil background produces an eerie effect when used with black construction-paper cutouts.

Sand painting was a ritual used in healing by the medicine men of certain Indian tribes. Intricate and beautiful designs were made using colored sand and powdered charcoal for color.

Children will need construction paper or a lightweight cardboard as a background for a sand painting. Sand can be colored by adding some dry tempera powder and mixing it well. Other materials such as dried coffee grounds, crunched eggshells, or small seeds can be used.

After the child draws a design on the background paper, he can

Sand painting

paint an area of the design with white glue (this will be easier to apply if the glue has been thinned with a bit of water first). He then sprinkles the sand or the other material over the glued area. After the glue has dried, the excess sand can be brushed off. All areas of the same color should be done at one time and allowed to dry before another color is applied, otherwise some of the colors may blend.

Spilled sand can present a cleanup problem, so you may wish to save this project for a nice day when it can be done out of doors.

Reverse painting

Tinsel painting

Prints with plaster block

Christmas tree decorations

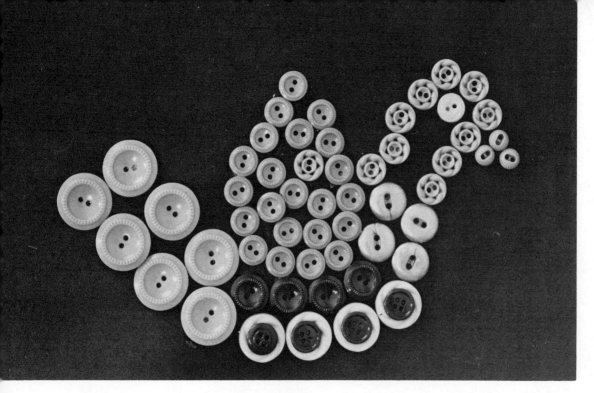

Button picture using various sizes and colors of buttons on a background of colored cardboard

Buttons provided another material from which to make unusual pictures. Some of the old button pictures had very intricate patterns and were surprisingly lovely.

To support the weight of the buttons, use a cardboard background. Provide a variety of buttons for the child to use. Let him develop his design according to the kinds of buttons he has available. Often the shape, color, or texture of a button will suggest a particular subject to him. After he has arranged his design, he can then glue the buttons to the background.

The early settlers enjoyed decorating their handmade items. With their limited materials they were quite inventive in their methods. And their simple decorations made everyday things more pleasing to look at and added a personal touch.

Thumbprinted gift box

One method of decorating was called the thumbprint. A painted object, such as a box, was covered with a pattern of thumbprints made in a contrasting color. The prints might be at random, or form a definite pattern.

Any plain-colored box will serve as a base for thumbprinting. The child applies the prints using a washable paint such as acrylic. Before beginning on the box, he should practice getting a clear print on a piece of paper. Have him dip his thumb into the paint, dab lightly on a paper towel or sponge to remove the excess, then press onto the paper, leaving a print. He may also wish to experiment using his other fingers, and forming designs with the prints. After a little practice, he will be ready to start on the box. Children will also enjoy printing some paper to be used for gift wrapping.

Shell decorating. The large box has
whole shells glued on. The oval candy tin
is covered with shell pieces.

35

The printed box makes an unusual gift box, and all that is needed is a ribbon to complete the wrapping.

Another method of decorating boxes, popular many years ago, was to add shells. A variety of shells glued to the surface of a box turns it into something special. Shells can be found at the seashore of course, but there are also some to be found along riverbanks. Some children will like to collect smooth, colored pebbles to use with, or instead of, the shells.

A small box (bath-powder boxes are very good for this) can be painted with spray paint or latex paint, and then the shells or pebbles arranged on the lid. When the child has a design that pleases him, he can glue the shells or pebbles in place. He now has a special box in which to keep his treasures, or to give to mother in which to keep some of her favorite things.

Printing is always fun for children, especially if they can print a picture of their own design. Woodcuts are pictures printed with carved wood blocks. A similar effect can be achieved by using a plaster

Plaster block
and print

of paris block instead of wood, and scratching in the design rather than carving. Mix the plaster according to the directions on the package and pour into a flat pan or box of the desired size. A plastic container or a small milk carton, cut in half lengthwise, will work well. After the plaster has set, it will be firm but still damp; it can be turned out and is ready for carving. Use the bottom side of the block for the printing surface, as it is the smoothest. For the carving use a pointed tool such as a large nail. After scratching in the design,

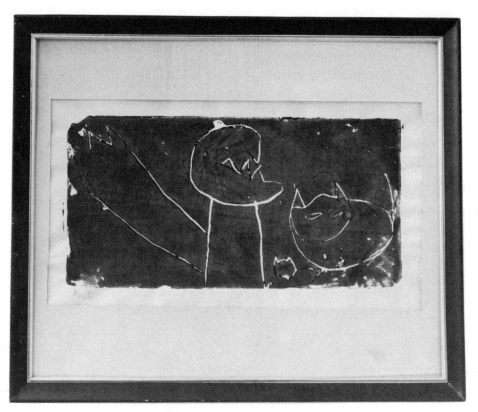

Framed plaster-block print

brush away the bits of plaster that are left on the surface, as the surface should be smooth to give a good, even print. The block should then be allowed to dry overnight.

When the child is ready to print his picture, the surface of the block should be first dampened with water to keep all the paint from being absorbed by the plaster. Then apply the paint to the surface of the block. A small roller, such as the one used in linoleum-block printing, works best. Applying the paint with a brush will also work fairly well. Tempera paint can be used and adding a little white glue to it will give it a slight gloss when dry. After the paint has been applied, place the printing surface on the paper to be printed and press down. Most any kind of paper will work, but brightly colored construction paper is particularly suitable. A pad of newspaper under the paper will provide a cushion and help in getting a good print. Separate the paper carefully from the plaster block to avoid smearing the paint and lay the print aside to dry. Have plenty of paper handy, as children will want to do a number of these prints. The best prints can be used to decorate greeting cards, or one can be framed to hang in the child's room.

Betsy Ross has been credited with making the first flag chosen to represent this young nation. Our flag today looks much the same as the first one, except the number of stars has changed as has the number of states in the Union. In addition to our national flag, each of the states has its own flag, and many clubs and organizations also have their special flags. Perhaps your child would like to make a flag. Colorful flags can be easily made from construction paper and glue or tape. Your child may wish to make the "Stars and Stripes," or

Construction-paper flags

perhaps the flag of his state, or maybe even one of his own design to fly at the door of his room or fort.

A Kachina doll

Kachina dolls represented the gods or spirits of certain Indian tribes. Each single Kachina, and there were many, had its own special costume and was important to a particular aspect of the tribe's history or religious beliefs. These dolls were made for the children of the tribe so they might become familiar with the legends.

The basic materials to make a Kachina are a paper tube, brightly colored construction paper, feathers, and glue. You may wish to provide additional items such as beads, ribbons, toothpicks, and corks. The child can use these materials to make a Kachina doll of his own design and perhaps even make up a story about his doll.

Spirits or luck have long been credited or blamed for the various things that happen to people. Some people believe that hex signs warded off bad luck, and there are special hex designs to bring luck, rain, love, happiness, and other desirable things. Whether or not they really do bring these things, they are certainly lovely to see and fun to make.

A compass is the only tool required, along with paper and some felt markers or crayons. Children who have never used a compass

Hex signs

will need to be shown how and encouraged to practice a bit. The design shown is simple enough for even a beginner. Set the compass indicator at 3 inches, or spread the compass apart until the pencil point and the compass point are 3 inches apart. Draw a circle. Now place the compass point at any place on the circle and turn the compass to make a curved line from one side of the circle to another. Move the compass point to the place where the line meets the circle and again turn the compass to make another curved line through the circle. Repeat this at each place where a line meets the circle. When finished, there will be a six-petal flower shape in the circle. To make a twelve-petal flower, repeat the same process to make another six-petal shape, only this time place the compass point halfway between two of the first petal points. After completing the drawing, the child can color the petals and mount the finished design on colored construction paper.

Christmas has always been a holiday which children have eagerly awaited. Early American children hung up their stockings with hopes of receiving a candy stick or toy—and certainly not the stick or switch that was left for children who had not been good. A holiday dinner, shared with friends and relatives, made it a joyous occasion.

Making decorations for a Christmas tree such as might have been enjoyed in America's early days is limited only by imagination, for decorations then were made from whatever materials were available. Children today will enjoy making gingerbread cookies, to be decorated and hung on the tree. They are not only pretty to look at, but smell delicious.

Bows made from strips of brightly colored calico or ribbon (about 8″ by ½″) add a colorful touch to the tree, as do pine cones striped with paint.

A stamp decoration is simple to make and it is one children may

Christmas tree ornaments

wish to keep year after year. Save Christmas stamps, postage stamps as well as those sent out by charitable organizations, and glue these to an appropriately shaped piece of colored cardboard. Since different designs are used for these stamps each year, the child can save some from each successive year and with each one the special memories of that year.

Quilled curls and paper stars are simple, and pretty, additions. And don't forget a paper star for the top.

Probably the most familiar of the decorations is the popcorn and cranberry rope. These are as much fun to make as they are to see, and it makes a great evening project for the entire family. You will need to make two batches of popcorn for this—one for eating and one for stringing! Stale popcorn works better for stringing as the kernels do not break apart as easily, so you may want to make this batch early in the day. Use tapestry needles which have a blunt end and long pieces of heavy thread for stringing the popcorn and cranberries (use only the firm berries). Some apple cider and Christmas carols are the only other things needed to make it a most enjoyable evening.

2.

Stitching and Weaving

In the early days of this country, getting a new shirt or dress began with the growing of cotton or flax or the raising of sheep. It was a long and difficult procedure to even get the fibers ready for spinning —one that involved all members of the family. After the fibers were spun into yarn, they could then be woven into the cloth from which to make the clothes.

The yarn or cloth was dyed with colors obtained from plants, fruits, vegetables, and flowers. These natural dyes produced soft colors, not as bright as the prepared dyes available today. The colors for natural dyes come from a wide variety of sources, and only a few are listed here. After trying these, you may wish to experiment with other vegetables and flowers to get other colors.

To produce a yellow-orange dye, remove the dry, colored skins from onions. Pour enough warm water over the skin to cover them,

and simmer over low heat for about thirty minutes. Strain to remove the skins.

A red can be obtained from beets. Finely chop raw beets and proceed as for the onion skins.

Walnut shells can be covered with warm water and allowed to stand overnight. This will extract the brown color from the shells. A light brown dye can be quickly made by adding one-half cup of instant coffee to one quart of hot water.

Grape juice can be used for a lavender color.

A tablespoon of vinegar added to any of these dyes will help to strengthen them. The fabric or yarn can be dyed by dipping it into the dye solution, but you achieve the best colors if the fabric or yarn is allowed to simmer for a time in the dye. The fabric or yarn should be dampened before placing it in the dye solution, and after dyeing should be rinsed with cold, clear water.

In colonial days, sugar came wrapped in a dark blue paper. This paper was carefully saved, then soaked in water to extract the coloring from the paper. You can use this same method to extract the color from crepe paper. Place pieces of crepe paper in a bowl, and pour warm water over them. Allow this to sit for about ten minutes and then strain. Again, add a little vinegar to strengthen the dye. Colors obtained this way are brighter than those from natural sources, but they aren't as much fun to make.

Perhaps your child will want to experiment with tie-dyeing while using these dyes. An area of the cloth can be twisted and tied with string (or simply use a pinch-type clothespin to hold the fabric) to prevent the dye from penetrating that area. Some unusual starburst effects result from this procedure. Small placemats, napkins, or handkerchiefs can be dyed in this manner and make handsome gifts.

Some of the dyed yarn can be used for weaving. The first step is to construct a simple loom. A small cardboard box, such as processed cheese comes in, will serve as the loom. A row of nails placed in each end will hold the warp threads in place. For the warp threads, use string or yarn, and make a loop in one end. Place this loop over the first nail on the lower left, then run the thread up to the top, around behind the nail, down to the bottom, around the second nail, up to the top again, and so on. When the last nail is reached, again make a loop and slip it over. Now the loom is ready for weaving.

The child can make a shuttle for holding the yarn while weaving

—this not only keeps the yarn clean, but also keeps it from getting tangled. One can be cut from a 2″ by 4″ piece of cardboard, according to the pattern in the diagram. The end of the yarn is placed in the center slit to hold it, and the rest of the yarn is wound around the center of the shuttle.

Shuttle

To aid in the weaving, a tongue depressor can serve as a harness. Using the tongue depressor, go over the first thread and under the second—continue this over-and-under procedure to the other side. Now turn the tongue depressor on one edge so as to prop up the threads and give room for the shuttle to go through. On the next row go under and over the opposite threads with the tongue depressor and repeat the process.

One yarn can be woven back and forth for a desired distance and then cut off. The loose end is woven in along with the new yarn, and the end of the new yarn is also tucked in. For variety, after several strands have been woven in, the child can do some weaving only halfway or less across the loom. Then, with another color, continue the weaving by going all the way across. The upper edge of the weaving will now be uneven, so it can be filled in on the other side with yet another color. In the woven piece on the right side of the photograph the bottom area was done in this fashion. This way the child can create some unusual patterns.

Woven pieces and a braided rug. One piece was woven using single yarns. The one on the right uses continuous yarns.

Another method of weaving is to use single pieces of yarn. Each one is woven in and the ends allowed to form a fringe along the edges. The piece on the left side in the photograph was done this way. After weaving several strands, the child should use a coarse comb to push the weaving toward the bottom. This will keep the weaving tight and even.

On the last few rows there will not be room for the shuttle to go

Natural dyes—yarn, and
tie-dyeing

Pinpunch designs mounted on construction paper

Doll's quilt

Bread clay figures

A stocking doll and a spoon doll

through, so the yarn can be woven in by hand or with a large needle. When the weaving is completed, slip the woven piece off the nails. The two ends of the warp thread (the looped ends) should be tied to the next thread. Spread the woven area to fill the space to the ends of the warp threads. If single yarns have been used, knot the fringe along the edges to keep the weaving in place.

Attached to a twig or small dowel, these weavings make attractive wall hangings.

Old clothing was frequently cut into strips and braided to make rugs. These thick colorful rugs were a welcome addition to the early homes. A child can easily make a small braided mat or rug using leftover pieces of double-fold bias tape. Knot three pieces of the bias tape together, and let the child braid these. Stitch on a new length as it is needed. The more colors of tape, the better. When he has braided the length he wants, the end of the braid can be knotted. The braid can now be coiled into a circle or an oblong shape. These coils can be sewn together or glued to a cardboard backing. The end can be stitched to the bottom side of the rug, or tucked under and glued in place. This makes a perfect rug for a dollhouse, or a mat on which to set a vase of flowers.

Spool knitting was done many years ago, using an empty thread spool and thread. This was a slow, tedious process, and the resulting yarn was very fine. This can be more easily done using a wooden curtain ring (2½ inches in diameter), five small brads, a crochet hook, and heavy yarn. Using these materials, the knitting goes along quite rapidly. It will be easier for the child if you mark where he

50

Place brads at each of
the five points

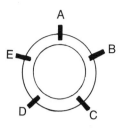

should pound in the brads on the ring. The placement of the brads is shown in the diagram.

1. Begin winding the yarn at brad B.
2. Wind the yarn around B, then around D, to A, to C, and then to E. This forms a star shape.
3. Form a second star over the first, again starting at B, in the same manner as before.
4. Using a crochet hook, pull the lower loop up and over the brad, and release it. Work all the way around the star.

Step 1. Beginning the winding

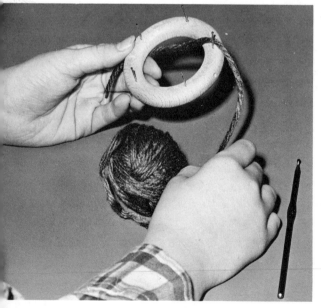

Step 2. Producing a star shape

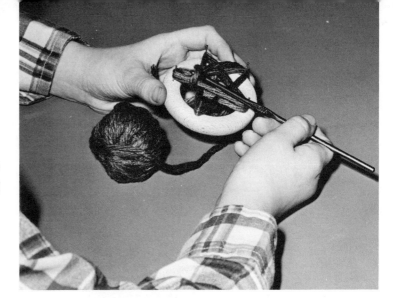

*Step 4. Pulling lower loop
up over the brad*

5. Repeat steps 3 and 4 until the desired length is knitted.
6. To finish the rope, cut the yarn, allowing 5 inches for tying. Pull the loose end through each of the star points. Tie the end of the yarn into the rope.

*Step 5. Continue forming stars and knitting each point
to form the knitted braid.*

Spool-knit rug

A child can change colors of yarn at any time, simply by tying on a new color and continuing the knitting, pushing the knot to the inside of the rope. After the rope is completed it can be coiled and sewn together with heavy thread. Depending on the length of the rope, the child will have a hot pad, a placemat, or a rug.

A God's Eye is made by winding yarn on sticks to form a pattern. This is traditionally done using brightly colored yarns. The base is two sticks or dowels of the same length. Sticks that are between 8 inches and 12 inches long make a good size for the beginner. Lay one stick in a vertical position and place the center of the second stick crosswise over the center of the first. The position of the sticks is that of a plus sign. The beginning yarn should first be tied around the sticks at the center, where they meet. Then begin the weaving by going across the front of one stick, around behind it, and across the front again and over to the next stick. Continue weaving around and around until an area of color has grown to the desired size, then tie on a new color of yarn and continue the weaving. The ends of the stick can be wrapped with yarn, and several pieces of yarn can be added for tassels if desired.

God's Eyes

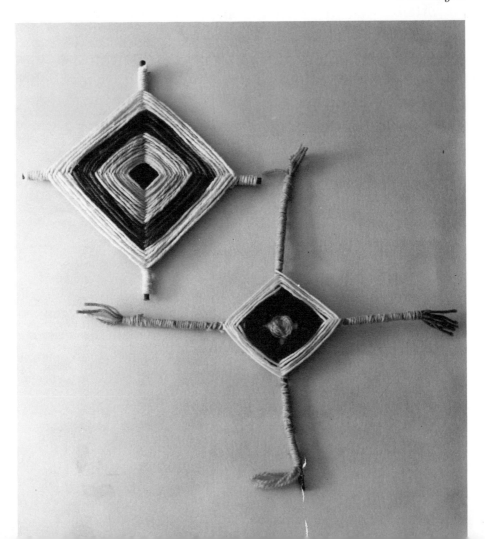

Pinpunch embroidery was often used to make bookplates or bookmarks. This type of embroidery, done on pieces of stiff paper, followed a pattern of pinholes which had been made in the paper to form the design.

White or colored construction paper provides a good background for pinpunch embroidery. The child will find it helpful if he sketches his design lightly on the background paper with a pencil, and then follows this design in making the pinholes. Bulletin Board pushpins are the best for making the pinholes as the heads are large and easy to handle—they also prevent sore fingers.

After the pinholes are made, and the pencil lines erased, he is ready to begin the embroidery. Stitching is done with a needle and thread or embroidery floss. There are two kinds of stitches to be used here: a straight stitch for a short, straight line, and a backstitch for a long or curved line.

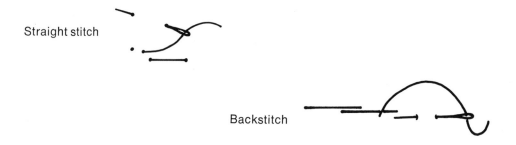

Straight stitch

Backstitch

All knots should be made on the back side of the paper, and the knots taped in place. After the stitching is completed, the designs may be mounted on construction paper. These little stitched pictures make handsome bookmarks, or can be used on a greeting card for a special friend.

Pinpunch embroidery

The samplers done by young girls many years ago generally contained the letters of the alphabet, numbers, and often a rhyme or religious verse. Girls were expected to know how to do very fine stitching, and samplers were their practice pieces. The little ladies took great care to do their very best in stitching these samplers. At the same time they were learning to make fine, delicate stitches, they were also becoming familiar with the letters of the alphabet and their numbers.

A very simple sampler can be made using a piece of stiff paper (such as lingerie paper) or lightweight cardboard (tag board). A piece about 5″ by 8″ is a good size. Print the letters of the alphabet and the numbers on the paper lightly with a soft lead pencil, so these lines can be erased later. With the lines as a guide, the child can begin

Cardboard sampler

stitching his sampler with a needle and thread or embroidery floss, using the same stitches used for the pinpunch embroidery. He may choose to use all one color, several colors, or even change colors every letter or two. Whenever one color is ended, a knot should be tied on the back side and taped to the cardboard to keep the sewing in place.

After the sewing is completed, erase the pencil marks and mount the sampler on a piece of colored construction paper. Add a piece of yarn or thread at the top so the child can proudly display his sampler.

After doing the alphabet sampler, the child may wish to stitch a sampler of his own design. The design may be anything he pleases, perhaps just a simple picture without any letters. Use a fabric background, such as felt, for this. Again, the design should be drawn on the fabric to serve as a guide for the stitching. An embroidery hoop will be a help here as it not only holds the sewing surface flat, but also keeps the stitches from being pulled too tight.

This sampler will require more time than the cardboard sampler,

Felt sampler

but it will be more rewarding for the child because it is his own design. Be sure to always encourage his efforts. When the sampler is finished, it can be mounted on a piece of cardboard or fiberboard and hung for all to appreciate.

Fabric scraps and worn-out clothing were saved and cut into pieces to be used in quilt making. Sometimes special memory quilts were made in which each piece of fabric came from something that had special meaning. Pieces were cut from what had been a favorite coat, a first school dress, mother's best dress, and father's Sunday trousers. Pieces were saved year after year until enough were gathered to make the quilt. These quilts were often given by mothers to their children as wedding gifts—and they came complete with family memories.

Perhaps your child can collect enough pieces to make a memory quilt. The quilt piece for beginning quilt makers should be about 4 inches square. Thirty-six of these squares are required to make a quilt about 20 inches square. This quilt also requires a piece of fabric for the backing (usually of a solid color), some stuffing (cotton or dacron batting or a piece of lightweight blanket), and some yarn for tying.

The quilt top will be six rows of six squares each. To begin making the quilt top, join two squares together with a running stitch. The stitching should be about one-quarter inch from the edge of the pieces. It is not terribly important to stick to this measurement, but

Running stitch

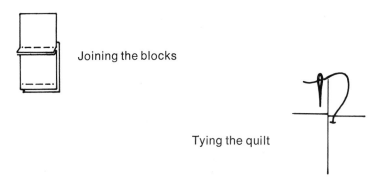

it is important that the seams be straight. At first it is helpful to draw a line on the quilt block as a guide for the stitching. This will help the child keep the seams fairly even. Continue to add blocks, always keeping the stitching on the back side of the row, until he has a row of six blocks. Then lay this row aside, and begin a new one. When all six rows are complete he is ready to put the quilt top together. Two rows are laid with the right sides facing each other (the "right" side being the one on which the stitching does not show). After stitching the length of the row, the rows are opened, and another row laid on for sewing. (Mother might wish to help here by machine-stitching the rows together—some unexpected help is always welcome!) After all six rows are sewn together it is time to join the quilt layers. First lay out the fabric for the backing, cover this with the stuffing, and then with the quilt top. Trim the edges of the quilt top if they are a little uneven. Pin the layers together in several places to keep them from slipping.

Quilting is stitching through all the layers in order to hold the two sides together and keep the stuffing in place. The simplest method of doing this is called tying. Use a large needle and yarn to do this. By doing the tying at the corners of the quilt blocks, the ties will be pretty evenly spaced. Start on the back side of the quilt and bring the yarn up through all the layers near a quilt-block corner. Go across the seam and down through the corner of another block. Turn the

Patchwork quilt

quilt over and tie the two ends of the yarn in a knot. Cut off the excess yarn, about one-half inch from the knot. Do this at each place on the quilt where four squares meet—or almost meet.

The final step is to bind the outside edges. Turn the edges of the quilt top and the quilt backing toward the inside, tuck in any stuffing, and stitch close to the edge. The child now has a lovely quilt for a favorite stuffed animal or doll, or just for himself to snuggle up to.

3.

Helping at Home

Children's help was welcomed, and sometimes necessary, in the many tasks common to early American households. There were crops and animals to be tended, food to be prepared for winter storage, candle making, soap making, as well as the daily activities.

Candles were made in the fall, so there would be a good supply for use during the winter, when the days are short. Candles were either dipped or poured, and it is fun to try both of these methods.

Dipping will produce a long, narrow candle, called a taper. It is made by simply dipping the wick into melted wax, allowing it to cool slightly, and dipping again—repeating this until the desired thickness is obtained.

The first step in dipping candles is to cover the floor and work surface with plenty of newspapers! The materials required are: wax, a dipping pan, cooking thermometer, and wicks. The wax should be candle wax rather than paraffin. This gives the best results and is safer and less smoky than the paraffin. Candle wax is quite economical if purchased in ten-pound blocks. If you have a supply of candle stubs, these can be melted and strained through cheesecloth for the wax supply.

The best type of pan to use is one that is deep and narrow, for the dipped candle will be only as long as the wax is deep. Break the wax in chunks for melting, and place in a double boiler or set the dipping pan in water in an electric frying pan. The latter is really better as it has a more controlled heat. The wax should be melted slowly over a low heat. When it has all melted and reaches a temperature of 160°F it is ready for dipping. The cooking thermometer is helpful here, so that you can adjust the heat to keep the wax within about 5°F of the proper temperature.

For each candle, the child will need a length of wick or white string about 3 inches longer than the candle is to be. To begin making his candle, he should dip the wick into the wax and lay it out on the paper. He can then straighten the wick by pushing his finger along it to the end. Let it cool until it is stiff (this will take only a minute or so). Now, he can begin dipping the wick into the wax, letting it cool slightly, and then dipping again. Caution the child always to dip the entire candle length into the wax (so that the wick touches the bottom of the pan), otherwise it will grow thick only at the bottom. He should also be sure to allow it to cool before dipping again. You will need to remind him about this, as it is such fun to see the candle grow with each dip that children tend to forget about the cooling. If the candle is dipped without enough cooling time, it will begin to get thinner instead of thicker. Should this happen, let the candle cool for

Dipping candles

several minutes before starting to dip again. After the desired thickness has been reached, the candle can be laid aside to completely
harden. Before using the candle, trim the wick at the top to about
one-half inch above the wax. For some candleholders it may be necessary to cut off the rounded portion at the bottom also.

A good way to use the remaining melted wax is to make poured
candles. Some of the early settlers did have candle molds, not of
course as varied as those available today. Any small can, such as a
juice can, will serve for a mold. The first step is to have the child
make a small hole in the center of the bottom of the can. Thread the

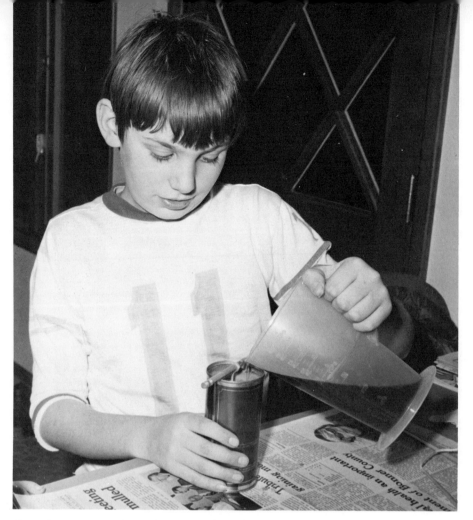

Pouring the wax into the candle mold

wick or string through this hole. Pull the wick through until it extends about an inch beyond the bottom of the can. Tape the wick in place on the bottom of the can, also covering the hole with the tape (this will prevent the wax from running out the bottom). Turn the can right side up and attach the top of the wick to a pencil with a piece of tape. Center the pencil so that the wick is straight. Now the mold is ready to be filled. It will be easier and safer for the child to pour if the melted wax is put into a pitcher. He should pour in enough wax to cover the bottom, and then wait a few minutes. As this cools, it will seal the hole at the bottom. Then add enough wax to fill the can almost to the top. Let the candle cool for about an hour. As the wax cools, it will shrink and leave a space at the top. This should again be filled with warm wax. Now the candle should be allowed to cool overnight. When the child is ready to unmold his candle, remove the pencil from the top of the can. Open the bottom of the can with a can opener, and place the can in warm water for a minute or so. The candle can then be slipped out. Remove the tape from the can bottom and slide the bottom off the candle. This end is now the top of the candle. Trim the wick, at each end, and the candle is ready to be lighted.

A word about cleanup is necessary. If the utensils used for candle making are to be used again for anything other than candle

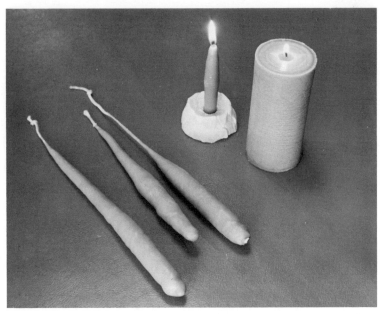

Dipped and poured candles

Candle box

making, they must be well cleaned to remove any bit of leftover wax. After using, wipe the utensils several times with paper towels. Rinse them several times with very hot water, and dispose of the water in a suitable place outside or in the garbage can. Scour the utensils thoroughly with a steel soap pad and rinse well.

When candles supplied most of the lighting in a home, they were treated with great care. They were carefully wrapped and stored in a cool dark place to keep them from becoming discolored. A few were kept handy in a candle box, which was usually made of tin, and hung on the wall or mantle. Perhaps your child will want to make a candle box in which to store his candles. A round box, such as an oatmeal carton, makes a fine base. First, tape the lid in place, and then cut a flap for an opening in one side. Paint the outside of the box with tempera, acrylic, or latex paint. When this is dry, he may want to paint a design on the outside. Punch two holes in the back side (opposite the door) through which to string a piece of yarn for hanging. He may also wish to add a yarn handle to the door. With his candles placed inside, the candle box is complete.

A child can also make a number of candleholders in which to

Tin-can lantern

burn his candles. One is a punched tin lantern, similar to those used many years ago. He will need a large can, a round foil frozen food container large enough to fit over the top of the can, and some wire.

Remove the label from the can, if there is one, fill the can with water, and freeze it. When the water has frozen solid, the can is ready to have holes punched in it. Lay the can on its side on a heavy towel, and using a hammer and large nail, punch holes in the sides of the can. These holes can be at random or form a design, whichever the child wishes. The holes should be at least one-half inch from the bottom of the can, otherwise melted wax from a burning candle may run out. If the can is very large, the bottom may bulge during freezing. Should this happen, pound it back into place. After punching holes in the lantern, punch holes in the "lid." Several holes will do. Punch one fairly close to the rim. Run a piece of wire through this hole and through a hole in the lantern and twist the ends together. This will serve as a hinge for the lid. Attach a small loop of wire through two holes near the top, on opposite sides of the can. A length of wire can now be attached to these loops for a handle. The child can then place a candle, a wide one such as those he poured, inside the lantern. This lantern should not be carried while lighted unless the handle extends 12 inches or more above the lid. The lighted lantern casts soft patterns of light through the punched holes.

Other types of candleholders can be made from baker's clay or bread clay. Following the recipe directions, a child can construct most any kind of candleholder he desires.

BAKER'S CLAY

4 cups flour
1 cup salt
1½ cups water
Food coloring, optional

Mix the ingredients and knead well. If the dough is too sticky, add a little more flour. Shape the candleholders and place them on a foil-covered cookie sheet for baking. Bake at 250°F until firm—usually about two hours.

The recipe for bread clay requires bread crumbs. Fresh bread crumbs work best, and these can be quickly made by whirling some small pieces of bread in a blender for a few seconds. Add powdered tempera to produce a brilliantly colored dough. It can be mixed in with the bread crumbs, or worked into a portion of the kneaded dough.

This clay can be molded and then left to dry. It dries very hard, without baking, and retains its bright color. Bread dough does not stick to itself as well as does the baker's clay, so separate pieces of the object you are making may have to be glued together with white glue after drying.

BREAD CLAY

2 cups fine bread crumbs
4 tablespoons white glue
2 teaspoons vinegar, or lemon juice
Powdered tempera, optional

Combine the ingredients and knead well. After kneading, the dough should be fairly stiff but smooth. If it is too dry, add a few drops of water. After shaping, allow to stand for several hours until hard and dry.

Children will particularly enjoy this clay, because of its pleasing texture and bright colors. Don't be surprised if they begin making a lot of things besides candleholders. Whatever they make, they will most certainly have a good time—which is the most important thing.

Bread-clay duck

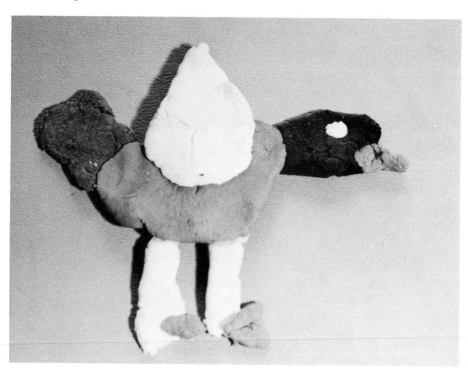

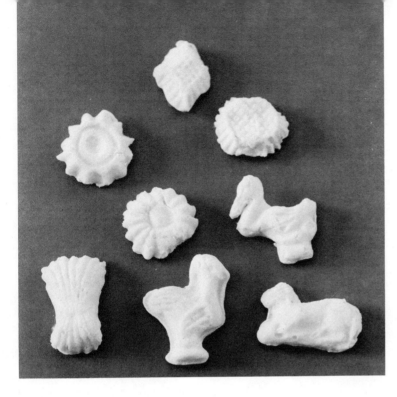

Soap bars made in cookie molds

In the early days, families made their own soap by combining grease and lard with lye. This mixture required long cooking and frequent stirring over an outdoor fire. Soap making was not an activity that children enjoyed, for they often had the job of stirring the soap. It was a tedious process, for it had to be stirred just right and watched carefully.

Children of today can make some soap of their own, using a shorter and much safer process than was used then. They should save all the leftover bits of hand soap, which are often thrown away. The slivers can be cut up or grated and mixed with an equal amount of water. Allow this mixture to sit overnight in order to soften the soap pieces. After the pieces are softened, the mixture is ready for cooking. The mixture should have the consistency of thick pudding, so add a little water if it is needed. Cook the soap over low heat, stirring constantly, until it is smooth and clings together in a ball. At this time it is ready to be shaped into cakes. It can be pressed into

muffin tins or small cookie molds. It also can be patted out and, after it has cooled a bit, cut with cookie cutters. After the soap has been allowed to harden overnight, it is ready to use.

Old-fashioned cookie cutters were generally made of tin, and often in fancy designs. If you're making cookies, why not let your child make some cookie cutters of his own design to use. The cutters can be made from strips of plastic, cut from large plastic bottles (make sure these bottles have been thoroughly cleaned if they contained a substance such as bleach). Overlap the ends of the strip, to form a circle, and tape together. The child can bend these circles into various shapes, and crease them where necessary to hold the shape. These can then be used to cut some unusual cookies from the cookie dough.

Children find cooking particularly enjoyable. Perhaps they will want to try making cornbread, according to your favorite recipe, or baked apples. Both of these were popular with the early Americans. You might also want to try making butter from cream, but don't forget to add a bit of salt and yellow coloring. The colonists often drank tea made from the dried leaves of various plants. Some of the popular ones were blackberry, mint, catnip, strawberry, and currant. These are fun to try—just be sure the plants have not been treated with any poisonous fertilizer or spray before using them for tea. And don't forget popcorn, or parched corn as it was known then.

Gardening was another home activity in which children took part. The garden was very important to those early families. It not only supplied much of the food, but it also provided the herbs and spices for cooking and for the family's medicine. It was frequently the responsibility of the children in the family to care for the garden.

Maybe your child would like to start a little garden of his own. A window garden is particularly good for beginners. First, the child will need to decide what kind of plants he wishes to grow. Perhaps, like in the early gardens, he may wish to grow herbs. Most herbs grow well in window gardens, and some have a pleasant aroma.

Small pots, or milk cartons cut in half lengthwise, will serve as the garden. Fill the pots with soil, or put several inches of soil in the carton. Make small holes in the soil, about one-quarter inch deep, in which to put the seeds. Spread the soil gently to cover the seeds and then sprinkle with water to thoroughly dampen the soil. A laundry sprinkler is good for watering as it sprinkles droplets of water rather than a stream of water, which is likely to wash out the seeds. If the small pots are used, a saucer or plastic meat tray should be placed under the pot to hold any excess water. Be sure to check the seed packet for the germination period, so the child will have an idea of when to expect to see the first sprouts. Help him to remember to water his garden regularly.

4.

Indoor Toys
and Games

Rainy or snowy days mean children will spend more time than usual indoors. On days such as these, it is fun for them to have something a little different to do. How about an old-fashioned game, which they can make themselves?

Checkers is a favorite children's game, and one which is simple to make. The checkers can be thread spools or buttons. Each player needs twelve "men" of the same color. If thread spools are used, color one end with a felt marker and make an X or a crown on the other end so it can be turned over for a king. Buttons can also be marked on the back side with felt markers to make a king. To make the board, use construction paper or a lightweight cardboard, such as tag board or poster board. A good size for the board (which must have 64

*Making the checker board using the uncut strip for a pattern
in placing the blocks*

squares) is 12″ by 12″, thus making each square 1½″ by 1½″. To form the checkerboard, the child will need thirty-two squares of a contrasting color. These can be made from four strips of paper 1½″ by 12″. Mark the strips to form 1½-inch squares. The child can then cut three of the strips, leaving one of the strips uncut to use as a pattern for laying the blocks. Lay the uncut strip across the bottom of the board, and begin gluing the cut blocks on the board in checkerboard fashion. After several rows are completed, the uncut strip can be cut into blocks, and the remaining blocks glued in place. As soon as the glue has dried, the game can begin.

This same procedure can be used to make a tic-tac-toe board. For this, the board will need to be only 4½″ by 4½″ to allow for nine squares 1½″ by 1½″. Mark the spools with an X or an O, or simply use different colors of buttons. There should be five markers for each player. Since there are nine squares, the one to play first will have five turns, while the one to play second will have only four. The two players can take turns being first.

Both checkers and tic-tac-toe are simple games to make, but they are certain to provide many hours of enjoyment.

Tops are good indoor toys, and if there are several children they can have some exciting contests to see whose top will spin the longest. To make a top, cut a circle from cardboard or a plastic coffee can lid about 3½″ inches in diameter. Clear or light-colored circles can be decorated with felt markers, which often make pretty patterns while spinning. A pencil (or a wooden skewer if you have one) is pushed through the center of the circle so that it extends about 1½ inches below the circle. The top is now ready for spinning. After spinning the top several times, the child may wish to see if he can lengthen the spinning time by changing the position of the circle on the pencil. Ready for a contest—ready, get set, spin!

Tops

Dancing bears and a snake

Some very amusing toys can be simply made from construction paper or cardboard and paper fasteners.

Even the youngest child can make the two dancing bears perform. By holding onto the bodies, one in each hand, and then moving his hands, he makes the bears' arms go up and down as they come together or part in their dance. To make the bears, cut two body shapes, two head shapes, two front legs, and four back legs of cardboard. Attach the parts with paper fasteners. Overlap the front paws and attach them with another paper fastener and the bears are ready to dance.

The snake is made in much the same way. The various pieces are connected at the "joints" with paper fasteners. Felt cut in a "V"

Running horse and flying bird

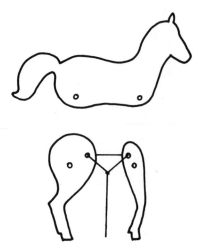

Make two holes near the
inside edges of the leg pieces,
and connect with a string.

makes the forked tongue. Take him by the head and the tail with both hands and push back and forth and the snake will wriggle.

The horse and the bird are two toys that move by a pull of the string. They are constructed the same way as the other toys, except that here the two moving pieces are connected by a string. By pulling the string first up and then down, the horse appears to run and the bird appears to fly. The diagram shows how to connect the string.

These examples are just a few possibilities for moving toys. Your child is bound to come up with many more ideas of his own.

Flashcards are a learning aid that have been popular for many, many years, and are adaptable to any age. For the youngest children, ABC and counting cards are appropriate. Older children will find flashcards helpful in learning multiplication, division, or the capitals of states or countries. Plain index cards (3″ by 5″) are just the right size for flashcards. The "question" is put on one side, and the "answer" on the other. In this way, a child can use them by himself, turning the card over to see if his answer is correct. These are a valuable gift for a child to make for a smaller brother or sister.

ABC and counting cards

Spinners can be made in a few minutes, but will be played with for hours—by everyone no matter how old he or she is. Spinners require a button, a piece of string, and two one-inch plastic curtain rings. The button should be a two- or four-hole button, the heavier the better. If the button is quite lightweight, glue two together, making sure the holes match. The added weight will give a better spin. Provide a piece of string about 36 inches long. Have the child thread the string through one hole and then back through the other hole. If using a four-hole button, use two holes opposite each other. Tie the ends of the string together. Move the button to the center of

Spinner

the string, so that the loops are about the same length on each side of the button. Tie a plastic curtain ring at the end of each loop with a slip knot. To start the spinner, the child holds a ring in each hand, and twirls the button several times so that the strings are twisted. He should then jerk both hands outward, at the same time, and then move them back toward each other a little. Do this several times, and this should start the button spinning. He should then continue to move the hands out and in to keep it spinning. If it doesn't work the first time, twirl the button again and start over. It may take him a few tries to get the knack of spinning, but when he does he will be delighted. Some buttons make a gentle whirring noise when they get spinning rapidly, which adds to the fun.

Children in Colonial times often played string games and Cat's Cradle was the most popular. Children who are not familiar with string games should begin with one a little less complex than Cat's Cradle. Here is one called Seesaw, which is played by two children.

1. Use a 30-inch piece of string and tie the ends together. The first child makes a loop over the four fingers of each hand.

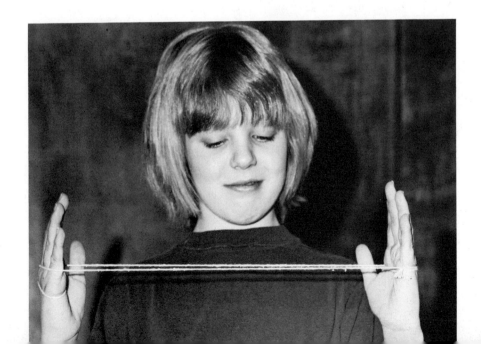

2. Insert the middle finger and ring finger of the right hand into the loop on the inside of the left hand. Pull the hands apart, and then do the same with the left hand—putting the two fingers through the loop on the inside of the right hand.

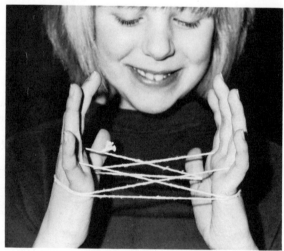

3. Pull the hands apart, and it should look like this photograph.

4. Now the second child takes hold of the two outermost strings.

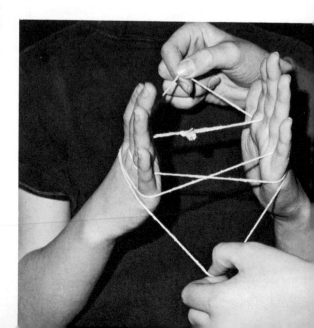

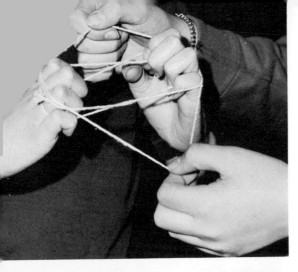

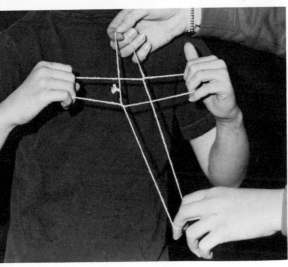

5. The first child bends his fingers, slipping out of the strings, but holding onto the loop around the two middle fingers.

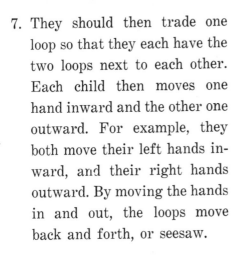

6. The string arrangement should look like this. The children are each holding loops which are opposite to each other.

7. They should then trade one loop so that they each have the two loops next to each other. Each child then moves one hand inward and the other one outward. For example, they both move their left hands inward, and their right hands outward. By moving the hands in and out, the loops move back and forth, or seesaw.

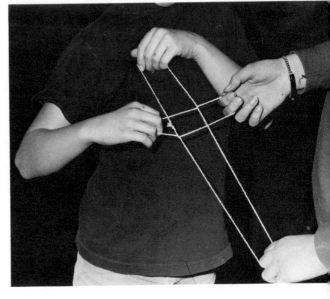

Dolls, or puppets as they were called, were lovingly fashioned from material at hand for the young children in the family. Dolls were made from such unlikely things as cornhusks, corncobs, sticks, and stockings. Decorated with pieces of calico, buttons, and yarn, these homemade dolls were warmly welcomed by the little ones in the family.

The simplest doll to make uses a stick, corncob, or even a wooden spoon. A felt marker, or pieces of felt, can be used to make the face. Add some dacron or cotton for the hair. A dress can be made from a large handkerchief or a square of calico. The handkerchief or calico should be folded diagonally, and placed on the head as you would a scarf. Wrap it around the doll and tie at the neck with a ribbon or piece of yarn.

A very cuddly doll can be made from a stocking. The child stuffs the stocking (from toe to heel) with dacron or cotton batting or old nylon stockings. The stocking is then tied closed at the heel with yarn, and tied with another piece of yarn to form the neck and head from the toe. The child can add stuffing or yarn for the hair and draw the facial features on with a felt marker, or perhaps he prefers button eyes for this doll. The dress is made from a rectangular piece of fabric and should be long enough to cover all of the stocking, and wide enough to provide some fullness all the way around the doll. The dolls in the picture required a piece 12″ by 24″. With a thread and needle the child stitches a straight running stitch along the top of the dress. Holding onto the ends of the thread, he gathers the material by gently pushing it toward the center. When the gathered material is the right size for the neck, he puts the dress on the doll and ties the ends of the thread together. All she needs now is someone to love and cuddle her.

Cornhusk dolls

Cornhusk dolls have a special charm all their own. Children will find crepe paper a good substitute for cornhusks. The texture looks like that of the husks, but crepe paper is much easier for a child to work with. To begin the doll, take eight pieces of crepe paper, each about 4″ by 8″. Stack all the pieces, gather them together at one end, and tie tightly with a piece of string. Take the top four pieces and fold them over (so that the tied portion is between the two layers) and tie again at the neck, thus forming the head. To make the arms use a small piece of crepe paper 4 or 5 inches square. Roll this piece up and tie it at each end. Again separate the body piece of the doll into two layers (four pieces in each layer) and slip the arms between the layers. Tie with string at the waist. If the doll is to be a lady, fluff out the skirt and trim it at the bottom so it is even. To finish the lady, take a strip of crepe paper about 1″ by 6″ and wrap it around the waist, up over one shoulder, down and around the waist again, up over the other shoulder, and tuck the end in at the waist. This last piece isn't necessary, but it gives the doll a finished look. If the doll is to be a gentleman, cut a slit up the center of the bottom and tie each side at the bottom to form the legs. In the color picture opposite page 96 the gentleman doll at the right has crepe paper fringes and braids which were taped on. The dolls can be left as they are, or the child can decorate them if he wishes. He can use a felt pen to draw on a face and hair.

These dolls are fun to make and fun to play with. Have plenty of crepe paper handy, as some children will want to make an entire family.

The amusing characters in the picture are egg people, made from egg-shaped hosiery containers. First open the container, and have

Egg people

the child push a piece of clay in the bottom half—this will add ballast and keep the people standing upright. Have a variety of decorating materials on hand such as bits of various kinds of fabric, stuffing, yarn, cotton wool, construction paper, ribbons, glue, buttons, and felt pens. Once children start making these, you will find that you're out of containers long before they're out of ideas. Children are really delighted with these doll characters. They will wobble around but still remain upright, which adds to their charm.

Scrimshaw was primarily the art of the whalers. The whalers, out to sea for many months, often spent their leisure time carving whalebone or whale's teeth. Sometimes they made useful items such as small tools, pie crimpers, needle cases, bowls, or boxes from the whalebone. Often they carved a picture on a whale tooth. These very striking pictures were often stained with lampblack or colored inks to enhance the beauty of the carving.

Whalebone and teeth are no longer used for scrimshaw in this country. In an effort to preserve the whale, the government no longer permits whaling.

Perhaps your child will want to try his hand at scrimshaw, using small plastic bottles or containers, or a block of paraffin. A nail or bulletin board pushpin will serve as the carving tool. Since the scratches on the surface of a plastic container do not show up very well, it may be helpful to first have him sketch his design with a felt pen (not the permanent type). After he has sketched the design on the bottle, he can scratch it into the surface using the sketch as a guide. After he has scratched in the design, it is ready to be stained. Lampblack or powdered tempera work well for staining. Lampblack

Scrimshaw

can be obtained by holding a china plate over the top of a candle flame. With his finger, the child takes a bit of the lampblack and rubs it well into the scratched area. The excess can be wiped away with a damp cloth. For the paraffin block, tempera works best, but the

Carvings on driftwood

excess will have to be scraped off. A table knife, scraped lightly across the surface, will do the trick easily.

A jackknife was a prized possession of children in the early days, for both boys and girls did carving and whittling. They made useful things like clothespins, tool handles, cheese molds, butter paddles, and brooms. Often they made extra brooms which they could sell to earn a few extra pennies. Small toys or animals whittled from small wood scraps were also popular projects.

Most children today are not as familiar with carving and whittling as children once were, so it is best to start them out with a soft wood. Driftwood is generally quite soft and often has an unusual shape which will suggest an animal or object. A litle carving or whittling is all that's needed to change the wood piece into their own good-luck piece. Some also make very interesting wall decorations.

Bowling was a popular game for children years ago, and one children today will enjoy.

The bowling pins are cut from 1″ by 2″ wood, in 5-inch lengths.

Bowling set

Ano Kato

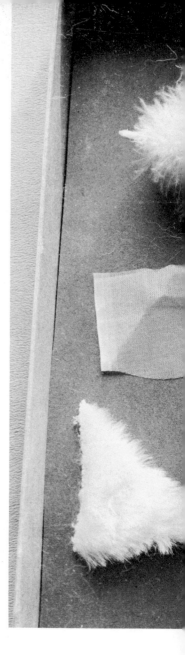

Your child will enjoy sawing his own pins with a handsaw. Wood scraps can usually be obtained from a lumberyard at little or no cost, and some of these pieces can be cut, or used as they are, for the pins. The length of the pins does not have to be 5 inches—a little more or less will work as well. The pins should be sanded to remove any rough

edges. All that is needed now is a ball. A baseball, softball, or a rubber ball will do fine. Now, let's go bowling.

Ano Kato was a most unusual game. Originally they were made with glass-topped boxes, but now one can make one with a box with a clear plastic lid such as a stationery box or a greeting card box. Inside the box place such things as bits of fur, feathers, wool yarn, cotton, and felt. Replace the lid. Using a piece of leather, fur, or wool, the child rubs rapidly on the surface of the box. The rubbing builds up static electricity on the lid, and causes the pieces inside to move and wave—some will rise up to the lid. The almost magical movement of the pieces in the box is certain to fascinate any child.

A family of cornhusk dolls

Egg people—a storekeeper, a bandit, and a patriot

Decorated kites

Weather vanes

5.
Outdoor Toys and Games

Toys and games that are really enjoyable aren't ever completely forgotten. Some fall out of favor for awhile, but are revived again and enjoyed as if they were brand-new.

Many of the old games are still popular with children. Every child has played at least some of the old games: leapfrog, tag, blindman's buff, London Bridge, hopscotch, marbles, fox and geese, and "Here We Go 'Round the Mulberry Bush."

There are many other tried-and-true games and toys that require equipment of a sort. Hoop rolling is certainly not the sport it was once, probably because barrel hoops are no longer a common item. However, a bicycle tire will work almost as well. The object is to keep the hoop rolling as long as possible. A stick can be used to keep the tire rolling, and also to control its direction. This offers

Coffee-can stilts

great fun for the beginner, and with a little practice he can become an expert. As might be expected, this is good exercise.

Another good outdoor activity is stilts. Part of their appeal to children is that suddenly they're taller and things all look different, even from a little way up. Some good stilts for beginners can be made from two two-pound coffee cans. Punch two holes, on opposite sides, near the bottom of the cans. Thread twine through the holes for the handles. You will need two lengths of twine, one for each stilt.

Thread the twine in one side of the can and out the other. With the child standing with one foot on each, bring the ends of the twine up to his hand, and tie the ends together. To walk on the stilts, each can is lifted up as a step is taken. These stilts can be used indoors as well as outdoors.

Spring weather is kite-flying weather, and this is one activity that has never lost its popularity. Kites can be made in most any shape, as long as you provide a good tail to hold the kite in a position to catch the wind. Directions are given for two kites, one in the traditional shape, the other a hexagonal shape. The paper for the kites can be butcher paper or wrapping paper. The kite sticks can be purchased from a hobby shop.

Kites

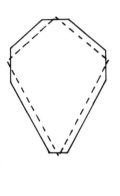

Traditional kite

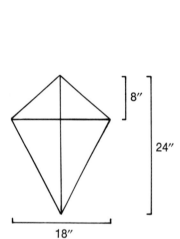

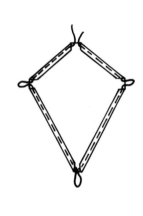

1. First draw the shape of the kite on the paper. Make a vertical line 24 inches long. Measure down 8 inches from the top and make an 18-inch line, across the first one (9 inches on each side of the first line). Connect the four points to form the kite shape.
2. Add 1 inch to each side of the kite, for folding. Cut the kite shape out, following the solid lines in the diagram.
3. Fold over the side edges. Place a piece of string all the way around the edge of the kite, under the folded edges, leaving a small loop at each point. Glue or tape the flaps in place.
4. Put the two sticks in place (each stick will need a small groove or slit in each end to hold the string). Slip the string into the slot at the bottom, and then each side. Pull the string so it is snug, and

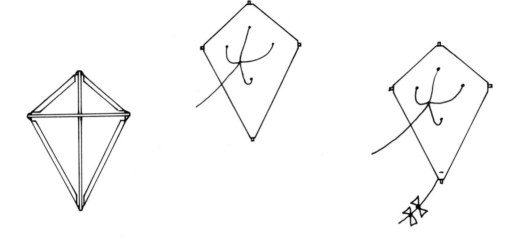

place the string in the top slot. Tie the two ends of the string together. Tie the sticks together at the center.

5. Now turn the kite over and attach the bridle. This requires two pieces of string 14 inches long. Attach one end of the string 4 inches from the end of one of the cross-sticks, go through the paper, around the stick, back up through the front and tie it. Do the same at the other end of the stick, using the other end of the string. Repeat this with the second string and the vertical stick, tying it 4 inches from the top, but tie it 11 inches from the bottom. Take hold of the two strings in the center and tie on the lead line (the one the child will hold onto to fly the kite).

6. The last step is to add the tail. The tail string is attached from the back side near the bottom of the kite. The string should go through the paper, to the front, across the stick and through the paper again to the back side. Tie the string. Tie several strips of fabric onto the tail string—leave plenty of string in case more tail is needed. A test flight will determine if the tail needs more strips.

The hexagonal kite is made in the same way as the traditional kite. It is a little more complicated because it requires three sticks instead of two.

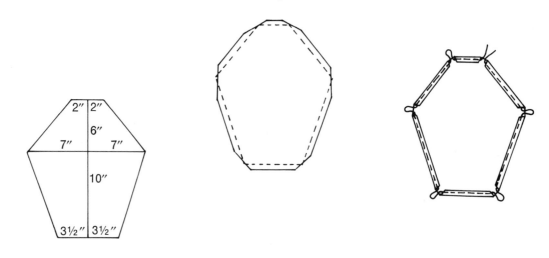

1. First draw the kite shape on the paper. Begin by making a vertical line 16 inches in length. Make a top line of 4 inches (2 inches on each side of the vertical line). Measure down 6 inches on the vertical line to make the second cross-line of 14 inches (7 inches on each side of the vertical line). The bottom line is 7 inches (3½ inches on each side). Draw in the four remaining sides.
2. Add 1 inch to each side and cut as shown by the solid lines.
3. Add the string under the folds and tape or glue the folds in place.

Hexagonal kite

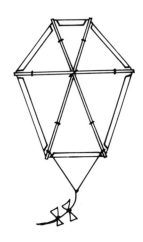

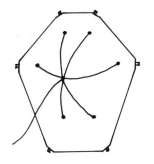

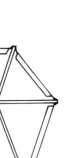

4. Attach the three kite sticks to the string loops at each point. Tie the sticks together at the center.

5. Using three pieces of string make the bridle. Tie the strings 2 inches from the top, 3 inches from the sides, and 4 inches from the bottom. Tie on the lead line as before.

6. To attach the tail, a piece of string is tied between the two sticks at the bottom, and the tail string is tied to the center of it. Tie on several strips of cloth. This kite will need more weight than the first kite because it is heavier—either use more pieces or heavier fabric. Again a test flight is needed to see if the tail needs adjustment.

Hobbyhorses—a horse and a Texas Longhorn

For a young horse lover, a trusty hobbyhorse is just the thing. It doesn't have to be a horse, of course—maybe your child would prefer to ride a Texas Longhorn, a Super Chicken, or an Elmer Elephant.

To make a hobbyhorse, cut two head shapes from lightweight cardboard (tag board or poster board). Add the desired features with a felt marker, yarn, or bits of felt. Staple the two head shapes together, leaving the neck end open. Insert a broomstick or large dowel into the neck end and push it into the head as far as it will go easily. Staple the cardboard onto the stick or dowel. Add some reins—and giddyup.

To make the Texas Longhorn, cut only one head shape from the cardboard. Cut the horns from another color of cardboard and glue them onto the back of the head piece. Glue the head shape to the end of a lunch-sized paper bag, and glue the reins in between the paper bag and the head shape. After the glue has dried, stand the bag upright and set in the broomstick or dowel. Stuff crumpled newspapers into the bag around the stick. Fill the bag about half full. Gather the upper portion of the bag around the stick (it's a good idea to apply some glue where the bag comes in contact with the stick) and tie tightly with string or cord. Okay, ride 'em, cowboy.

Maybe after a good ride, your child is ready for a quieter activity —like blowing bubbles. Make the bubble solution by adding three tablespoons of liquid soap to one-half cup of water and mix gently. The addition of a few drops of glycerin will make the bubbles stronger, so they will float farther before breaking. For the blower use canning jar rings, thread spools, pancake turners (the ones with long slits work better than those with small slits), straws, or a doughnut cutter. A check of the kitchen drawers may turn up other bubble makers.

There are a number of outdoor games children can make. Colonial boys often played a game called quoits, in which rope rings were thrown over a peg—the way horseshoes is played. To make a similar game, start with a number of plastic coffee-can lids. The child can cut either rings or horseshoe shapes from the lids. He then tosses these at a peg, which is simply a stick pushed into the ground. To play the game, children either take turns throwing the rings, or each child has his own set of three rings or horseshoes in different colors. Score two points for ringing the peg and one point for the ring or horseshoe closest to the peg. First to score fifteen points is the winner.

Playing catch has always been popular—how about trying basket

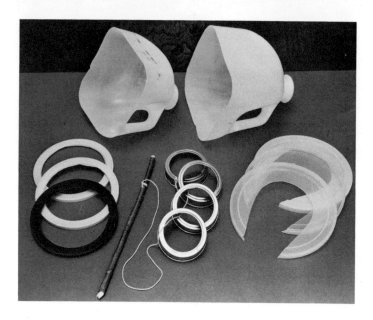

catch? Use the upper portion of a clean gallon-size plastic bottle. Use this to catch the ball, and it's not so easy as it looks!

Ring toss is an old game, but is still great fun. Use a stick or dowel about 12 inches long. Tie a string about 24 inches long onto the stick near one end. The rings can be canning jar lids, large curtain rings, or plastic rings. Thread three or four rings onto the string, and tie the end of the string to another ring. The child holds the stick, tosses the rings into the air, and tries to catch as many rings as possible on the stick.

There are several musical instruments which children can make easily. Perhaps after a little practice, they can form their own marching band.

A drum can be made from a two- or three-pound coffee can. Cut a piece of colored construction paper to fit around the outside of the can, and let the child draw some pictures or designs on the paper. The paper is then wrapped around the can and taped in place. A yarn handle can be added if desired. The drum has a better sound if it is played while it is being held by the handle.

A shoe-box guitar uses rubber bands to make music. First cut a hole in the lid of a shoe box (any size) and then tape the lid in place. Glue a "bridge" onto the box near the hole. The bridge will keep the rubber band from lying directly on the surface of the box, thus giving a better sound. Two popsicle sticks or a pencil will serve as a bridge. When the glue has dried, the box can be painted. Most any kind of water-base paint will work, but tempera paint may rub off on hands and clothing so you may wish to use another kind of paint for the guitar. After the paint has dried, the rubber bands can be added. Different-width rubber bands give different sounds: narrow ones give higher notes than wide ones. The child will have a good time just choosing and testing the "strings."

A "triangle" can be made from a wire coat hanger. In order to

Coffee-can drum and shoe-box guitar

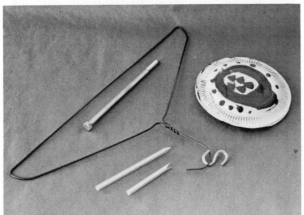

More musical instruments— a triangle, whistles, and a shaker

Cut a point in the flattened end of the straw.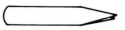

give a clear bell-like sound, the hanger should be held with an S-hook (or bend a paper clip into an S shape). The child plays the triangle with a large nail or bolt.

Whistles can be made from plastic drinking straws. Cut a piece of straw about 4 inches long, to make the whistle. Flatten the straw at one end and cut it to a point. This pointed end is the end which the child puts in his mouth. All that's left is to blow. It may take several tries before the child gets his whistle to "toot," but when he does he will be delighted. Whistles of different lengths will produce different sounds, so he may want to make several whistles in different lengths.

Shakers are made from two small paper plates stapled together with dried beans, peas, or popcorn inside to make the noise. These shakers can be painted with felt markers or tempera paint.

Weather vanes not only tell the direction of the wind, but are just plain fun to watch. A gentle breeze is all that's needed to make them turn. Here, a child's imagination can really be put to work. He can use most any kind of creature, real or fancied, or object for his weather vane. Disposable aluminum pans, colored plastic coffee-can lids, or sections of plastic bottles provide the material. These are all easily cut with scissors. Features or designs can be drawn on the aluminum or plastic with permanent felt markers.

An example of the simplest method of making a weather vane is the whale-shaped one in the picture. A single shape is cut from a disposable aluminum pan. In order to turn in the wind, the aluminum figure must be attached to a cap which can be slipped over the top of a dowel or stick. For the cap, use the top of a lipstick tube or an empty pill bottle, the tall narrow kind. Poke four holes through the aluminum shape—two on each side of the place where the cap will be. Wind a

Weather vanes—a simple whale, and more complicated ones with cross-sticks

pipe cleaner through the holes and around the cap, twisting the ends together, to hold it in place. Slip the cap onto the dowel or stick and let the wind blow. If the cap is placed off center, the heavier end of the weather vane will point in the same direction as the wind is blowing. The child doesn't need to wait for a wind either—just blow on it to make it turn.

A more complicated weather vane is made of two sticks and may have one or two figures. The figures are cut from disposable aluminum pans, and are attached to the ends of the cross-stick in an upright position. Use pipe cleaners to hold them on the stick. A thumbtack,

Placement of cap and holes
to fasten with a pipe cleaner

A thumbtack, pushed through the aluminum
into the dowel or stick, will keep the figure upright.

pushed through the aluminum into the stick, will keep the shapes standing upright. If the shape is tall (more than 4 inches) it may need a brace to keep it from bending over. The brace is a vertical stick, again attached with pipe cleaners. After both figures are in place, mount the cross-stick on the vertical one. The two sticks are joined with a thin finishing nail. A bead placed on the nail, between the two sticks, will keep the top stick turning easily. It is best to have an adult drill a small hole in the cross-stick for the nail. If this isn't practical, the nail can be pounded through. In this case, it is a good idea to wrap the stick or dowel with masking tape on either side of the spot where the nail goes, to keep the wood from splitting. After the nail is in place, the child should hold the nail with a pliers and turn the cross-stick around and around until it spins easily. Now, for the final step. Slip the bead onto the nail, and pound the nail into the top of the vertical stick. These weather vanes are larger than the first type, and really catch the wind, which sends them spinning.

*Attaching brace to the
back of a tall figure*

Pinwheel weather vane

Shaping the pinwheel

A pinwheel weather vane uses the plastic lid of a one-pound coffee can for the pinwheel. Follow the diagram, cutting on the solid lines, and bending on the dotted lines. The pinwheel is attached to one end of the cross-stick with a nail through the center of the pinwheel. Cut a tail from another lid or piece of plastic, and secure it to the other end with a pipe cleaner. This tail is to give the crosspiece good balance.

The weather vanes can be placed in the ground or wired to a fence post to turn whenever the wind may blow. There are many old sayings for forecasting weather, some of which concern the wind. For example: a wind from the east brings rain, or a wind from the east means the fish won't be biting that day. You probably know many other such sayings you could teach your child. It would be an interesting project for a child to keep a record of such weather signs and see how many of these old sayings really work—you may both be surprised at the results!

6.

Let's Pretend

Pretending comes naturally to children. Large boxes become houses, forts, or cars. An area under a porch or behind a hedge is a natural hideout. Hours can be spent playing house or school, or running a store or restaurant. Such play is always more fun if there are a few props to make it seem more like the real thing. In the following activities you and your child may find some new ideas for imaginative play.

A settlers' school would use hornbooks rather than textbooks, and quill pens instead of pencils. Since there were few books, each child had a hornbook from which to learn his letters. The hornbook was often made from a piece of wood, covered by a sheet of paper on which the letters were printed, and the surface was covered with a thin layer of horn.

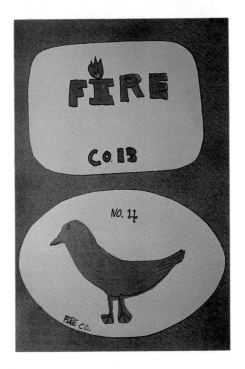

Fire signs

Log cabin scene

Totem pole

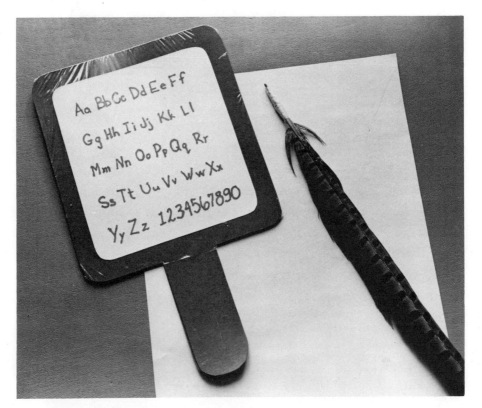

Hornbook and a "modern" quill pen

Your child can make his own hornbook, using two pieces of lightweight cardboard 6″ by 10″. Cut the two hornbook shapes according to the diagram. On a piece of paper 5″ by 5½″, draw the letters, and numbers if he wishes, and let the child go over the lines with a felt pen, or he may wish to draw the letters himself. After the lettered paper has been glued on the face of one of the hornbook shapes, this portion is covered with plastic wrap. The plastic wrap

Cutting the hornbook

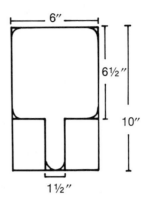

should be about one inch larger than the board, on each side. Wrap the plastic around the front of the board and tape it on the back side. Make a small cut in the plastic on each side of the handle to allow it to be folded over and taped on the back. The remaining flap, on the handle, can then be cut off. To complete the hornbook, glue the second cardboard shape to the back.

Writing was done with goose-quill pens and ink. Quill pens can be cut from most any type of feather you may have. With scissors,

Quill pens

a child can very easily cut a tip at the end of the feather. If you wish, you can slit the tip of the pen like an old-fashioned fountain pen.

 Tip of a quill pen

Since writing with pen and ink can be quite messy, and is not always satisfactory, your child may prefer something a little more modern. A ball-point pen cartridge can be slipped inside the "stem" of a large feather and taped in place. First snip off the end, so that the stem is large enough to accommodate the cartridge. Children are delighted with the results, for it is such fun to write with a feather.

Fire buckets were a necessity in early homes. They were special leather buckets, kept by the door and used whenever a building caught fire. When the fire call was heard, the men and boys responded. They formed two lines between the burning building and the well. The fire buckets were filled with water at the well, passed up one line, the water poured on the fire, and then the empty buckets were sent down the second line to the well to be refilled. When the fire had been put out, each man would take his bucket home and hang it up to be ready for the next time it was needed. These fire buckets usually had colorful designs, emblems, or crests painted on them, and each man could easily recognize his own bucket.

A child-size fire bucket can be made from a quart plastic container. He can paint his name or a design on the container with permanent felt markers. Punch holes in opposite sides of the container, and add a wire handle. Bell wire is good for the handle, as the plastic covering keeps it from rusting. A child's fire bucket won't

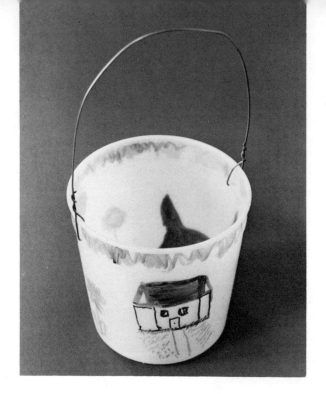

Fire bucket

Fire signs

be of much help putting out a fire, but he will certainly find other uses for it, like watering plants, playing in the sand, or maybe even carrying a picnic lunch to his hideout.

In the cities and towns there were groups of volunteer firemen who would respond to the fire call. If the burning building displayed a fire sign, it meant that the owner of the building had fire insurance, and the firemen would be paid for their fire-fighting efforts by the company named on the sign. The old fire signs were made of cast iron, and sometimes a brightly colored emblem was painted on the sign along with the name or number of the insurance company. These signs were given to the company's customers to be nailed to the insured building.

To make a fire sign, cut a background shape from construction paper or lightweight cardboard. The child can write the name or number for his company on the cardboard with crayon or felt pen. If he chooses to have an emblem, it too can be drawn on, or cut from colored paper and glued on.

The cabin in the photograph is made from corrugated paper, to give the appearance of logs. Construction paper forms the roof, and a long, narrow box, covered with construction paper, becomes the chimney. A bear skin of fur fabric is on a stretching board to dry. The pipecleaner lady is dressed in construction paper and bits of fabric, and is raking the yard. A covered well, an outdoor cooking fire, a worm fence, and pine trees (held in place with a lump of clay) complete the scene. Children may wish to add other things to their

A log cabin scene

scenes. A barn, a corral, animals, a stream, or a garden are just a few possibilities.

Corrugated paper can also be used to make a stockade. Maybe an Indian scene is more to your child's liking—try building a tepee, or a hogan from sticks and clay, or maybe a long house. While having a great time, children will also be learning a bit of history.

Dressing up in costumes is an important part of imaginative play. The tricorn hat, bonnet, and broom can be made by children who are pretending to be colonists. To make the tricorn hat, cut three pieces of black construction paper 5″ by 12″. Cut each in the shape illustrated in the diagram. Staple the three together so they fit the child's head, and add a feather or fancy button for decoration.

Tricorn hat pattern

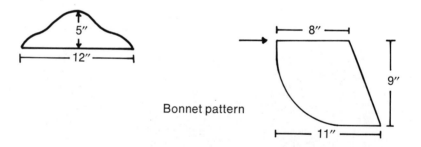

Bonnet pattern

A sunbonnet can be made from a piece of paper or calico that is 12″ by 18″. Fold the paper or calico in half and cut as shown in the diagram. Glue or staple the points together at the back, and add yarn ties to complete the bonnet.

A broom can be made from newspaper and a dowel or broom

Lay the newspaper along the dowel.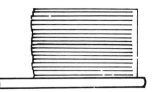

handle. Take four full-sized sheets of newspaper, stack them, and fold them in half crosswise. Fringe the folded newspaper to within 2 inches of the fold. After the fringing is completed, lay the edge of the newspaper along the handle, with the fold near the bottom end of the dowel, and the fringes extending toward the upper end of the handle. Apply glue to the length of the newspaper, near the fold. Wrap all the newspaper around the handle. Tie the newspaper in place tightly with string. Turn the broom right side up and gently pull the strips down into place. Tie another string around the strips near the top. Shake the broom to fluff it and it's ready to sweep.

Tricorn hat, bonnet, and broom

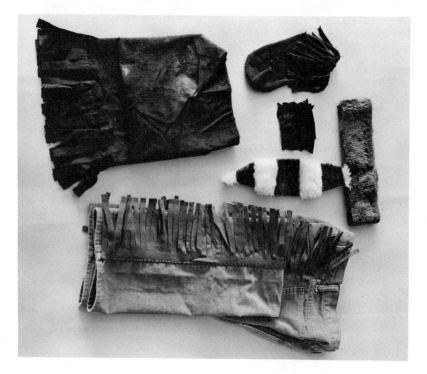

Frontier costume—
buckskin pants and shirt,
moccasins, powder pouch,
and coonskin cap

If the frontier life has captured your child's fancy, how about making a coonskin cap and some buckskins?

A coonskin cap can be made from construction paper or fur fabric. Cut a 2-inch-wide strip of paper or fur fabric long enough to go around the child's head and overlap a bit at the ends. Fit the strip around the child's head and staple it together. Now it needs a coon tail. Cut a 12-inch tail shape from paper, and glue on some dark and light stripes across the tail. Staple the tail to the back of the headband.

A buckskin shirt or dress can be made from a worn dark-colored pillowcase. Cut a 7-inch slit, on each side, near the top—the closed end—for armholes and an 8-inch slit across the top. Cut 6 inches down the center of the front, from the top, to allow for the head to go through. Fringe the bottom edge of the pillowcase.

Any pair of pants can become buckskins, simply stitch on some felt fringes down the outside of each pant leg.

Now, how about a pair of moccasins? Some can easily be made

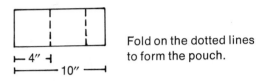

Fold on the dotted lines
to form the pouch.

from a pair of old socks. Cut fringes in the top part of the socks. A large rubber band around the ankle will help hold up the sock, if this should be a problem—just make sure it isn't too tight.

A powder pouch can be cut from a dark-colored piece of felt. Cut a strip 4″ by 10″. Fold over 4 inches at one end and staple, glue, or sew the side seams together. The top 2 inches form the flap. In order to carry the pouch, cut two small vertical slits in the back side; it can then be slipped on a belt or a strap over the shoulder.

The buckskin pants, shirt, and moccasins can also be used for playing Indians. Here, a headband with a feather will be more appropriate than a coonskin cap.

A necklace of wampum is not only pretty, but easy to make. Cut triangles from magazine pages—the more colorful the better. The base of the triangle should be about 1 inch wide, and the height of the triangle is the length of the page—making a very long, narrow triangle. The child rolls the triangle around a toothpick, starting at the base and rolling up the length of the triangle. Glue the tip in place, and lay it aside to dry while making another bead. When the bead is dry, slip it off the end of the toothpick. After the child has made a number of these beads, he can string them on a string and wear them as a necklace.

A young Indian brave will need a bow and arrows and maybe even a tomahawk. A green branch should be used for making the bow, as a dry one won't bend as well without breaking. The branch should be about 30 inches long and one-half inch in diameter. Tie a strong string or cord around one end of the stick. Bend the branch so it "bows" and then tie the string to the other end so it holds the

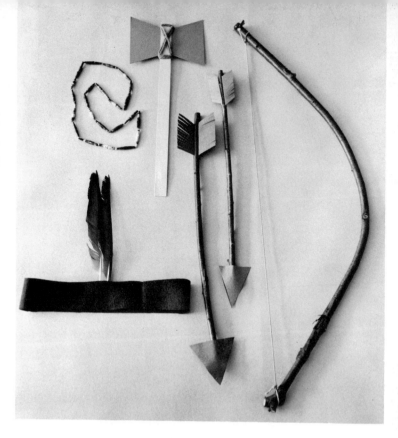

Indian gear—a headband, wampum necklace, tomahawk, and bow and arrows

bow shape. Now to make the arrows. The arrows are made from sticks about 18 inches in length. Glue paper triangles, one on each side of the end of the stick, for the arrow tip. Glue some paper feathers on the sides of the stick near the other end.

The head of the tomahawk can be cut from cardboard and stapled or glued to a cardboard handle. To make it look a little more authentic, wrap yarn around the head of the tomahawk.

What could be more fun for young Indians than a real tepee to play in? One can be very simply constructed from five cardboard tubes and several blankets. The cardboard tubes can be obtained (usually at no cost) from carpet dealers. For an indoor tepee, get 8-foot tubes or cut off the longer ones. If the weather is agreeable, the 12-foot tubes will make a larger outdoor one.

To make the tepee, gather the five tubes together and tie firmly

Indian tepee

with a rope about a foot from the ends of the tubes. Take the bundle of tubes and stand it upright. Then, one by one, pull the tubes away from the center, a little way at a time. Continue to move the tubes out farther until the tepee has the proper shape and a good amount of floor space inside. The final step is to cover the tepee with the blankets. To start, tuck one blanket corner into the rope at the top. Then run the length of the blanket down one pole and staple it to the pole. Wrap the remaining part of the blanket around the back and staple in place. Start the second blanket in the same place as the first, wrapping it in the opposite direction. Staple the second blanket only halfway down the pole, so that the lower part can be the door flap. Wrap the rest of the blanket around toward the back and staple in place. Depending on the size of the blankets used, and the size of the tepee, you will need one or more blankets to finish covering the spaces in the back side.

If you need to move the tepee simply gather it up, blankets and all, and set it up somewhere else. For an outdoor tepee, it's a good idea to have extra blankets or sleeping bags handy—your Indians will probably want to spend the night in it.

Totem poles were made by the Indians of the Pacific Northwest to show the lineage of a particular family, a kind of family tree. These carved poles used legendary birds and animals to show the family history.

The totem pole in the picture was made from eight two-pound coffee cans. The cans were stacked and taped together, then covered with butcher paper. The added decorations were cut from colored construction paper and glued in place. It's a good idea to put some sand or pebbles in the bottom can to give the totem pole stability. If

A totem pole made of coffee cans

you have a group of children, you may wish to give each one a coffee can which he can wrap with the background paper. Each child can then make his own design and all of them can be stacked and taped together. Whichever way it is done, the result will be a delightful and brightly colored totem pole.

INDEX OF PROJECTS